Thus Says The Lord Workbook

Devotional Workbook

Companion to Thus Says the Lord: 31 Days Devotional

By Nadia A. L. Farrington

Scripture quotations are taken from the King James Version (KJV) and American Standard Version (ASV) of the Bible, which are public domain.

THUS SAYS THE LORD DEVOTIONAL WORKBOOK

Nadia Farrington
Whispers at Sunrise
P.O. Box F44404
Freeport, Grand Bahama
Bahamas
www.whispersatsunrise.com
whispersatsunrise@gmail.com

ISBN: 979-8-9930641-1-6

Cover design by Nadia A L Farrington
Interior design by Nadia A L Farrington

Published by Nadia A L Farrington

Printed in the United States of America

Acknowledgements

I am deeply grateful to God for His Word, which gives life and light.

To my family and loved ones, thank you for your encouragement and support.

And to every reader who chooses to walk through this devotional journey thank you for allowing me to share in your faith walk.

Welcome Note

Dear Friend,

I want to personally welcome you to the *Thus Says the Lord Devotional Workbook*. My prayer is that as you journey through these pages, you will not only read God's Word but also experience it deeply in your own life.

This workbook was designed to be used alongside my book, *Thus Says the Lord: 31 Days Devotional*. Together, they create space for both inspiration and reflection helping you move from reading God's truth to living it out daily.

Think of this as your personal journal with the Lord. Each page is a conversation between you and Him. Don't worry about writing the "right" words just write honestly from your heart.

I believe the Lord will meet you here in these quiet moments. By the end of this journey, you will hold in your hands a testimony of what He has spoken to you, day by day.

Thank you for allowing me to walk alongside you in this season. I pray that your time with the Lord through this workbook strengthens your faith, renews your mind, and draws you closer to His heart.

With love and blessings,
Nadia A. L. Farrington

Table of Contents

1. Introduction 6

2. How to Use This Workbook 7

3. Daily Reflections (Days 1–31) 8 - 115

4. Final Blessing 116

5. Continuing The Journey 117

6. Prayer Tracker 118

7. Reflection Summary 119

8. Notes Pages 120

9. About The Author 122

10. Stay Connected/ Permission Credits 123

Introduction

Welcome to the *Thus Says the Lord Devotional Workbook*.
This workbook was created as a **companion guide** to the devotional book *Thus Says the Lord: 31 Days of Reflection in God's Word*. While the devotional offers you Scripture and encouragement each day, this workbook provides **space for you to respond** to pause, reflect, and put into writing what the Lord is speaking to your heart.

As you move through the Scriptures and daily messages, this workbook will help you:

- Deepen your personal connection with God's Word.
- Write out your reflections and prayers.
- Record what the Holy Spirit reveals to you each day.
- Build a habit of intentional time with God.

This isn't just a book to read, it's a space to grow. By the time you complete the 31 days, you will have a personal record of your walk with the Lord, filled with insights, lessons, and prayers that you can return to again and again.

How to Use This Workbook

1. **Read the Day's Devotional First**

   Begin with the corresponding entry in *Thus Says the Lord: 31 Days Devotional*. Read the Scripture and reflection thoughtfully.

2. **Pause and Pray**

   Before writing, invite the Holy Spirit to guide your thoughts and open your heart to what God wants to reveal.

3. **Reflect & Write**

   Each workbook page contains:
   - **Scripture focus**
   - **Reflective question(s)**
   - **Space to write your thoughts, prayers, and insights**

   Don't worry about writing perfectly. These pages are for you and God.

4. **End with Prayer**

   Conclude each entry by writing a short prayer, asking the Lord to help you apply His Word to your daily life.

5. **Stay Consistent**

   Work through one devotional and workbook page each day or move at a pace that works best for you. Consistency is more important than speed.

DAY 1

Forgiveness

Luke 17:3-4 KJV

> *Take heed to yourselves: If thy brother trespass against thee, rebuke him; and if he repent, forgive him. And if he trespass against thee seven times in a day, and seven times in a day turn again to thee, saying, I repent; thou shalt forgive him.*

What are your thoughts on today's devotion.

_____

_____

_____

_____

_____

Is forgiveness a struggle for you? _____

How do you plan on overcoming this struggle? _____

What is being said in your own words?

_____

_____

_____

_____

_____

_____

_____

_____

Make a list of insights that stood out to you and think about how to apply them in your daily life.

_____

_____

_____

_____

_____

Which ones can you use in your daily life.

_____

_____

_____

_____

Take a moment to reflect. What is God saying to you about forgiveness?

_____

_____

_____

_____

_____

_____

_____

Matthew 6:14-15 states that forgiving others is not just beneficial for them but necessary for us, it allows God to forgive us in return.

My Prayer Today

Conclude each entry by writing a short prayer, asking the Lord to help you apply His Word to your daily life.

_____

_____

_____

_____

_____

_____

Day 2

Prayer For a Tender Heart

Ezekiel 11:19 KJV

And I will give them one heart, and I will put a new spirit within you; and I will take the stony heart out of their flesh, and will give them a heart of flesh:

The term tender hearted is defined as being easily moved to love, compassion, pity or sorrow.

Define this term in your own words to demonstrate your understanding on today's devotion.

_____

_____

_____

_____

_____

What is the Bible verse above saying to us about God's promises?

_____

_____

_____

_____

_____

_____

_____

Why is it important to have a tender heart in our daily interaction with others?

_____

_____

_____

_____

_____

As we search within ourselves, let us remember to reflect deeply on today's scripture and find solace in its wisdom.

My Prayer Today

Conclude each entry by writing a short prayer, asking the Lord to help you apply His Word to your daily life.

_____

_____

_____

_____

_____

_____

_____

_____

Day 3

The Love of God

John 3:34 KJV

For he whom God has sent Speakes the words of God: for God gives not the Spirit by measure unto him.

What is Agape love?

_____

_____

_____

_____

_____

What are the different kinds of love described in today's devotion?

_____

_____

_____

_____

_____

John 3:16 states how much God loves us. How does this verse impact your understanding of faith and love? What does this mean to you personally?

_____

_____

_____

_____

_____

_____

Why are we told to love others unconditionally? Why are we told to love our neighbors as ourselves?

_____

_____

_____

_____

Let us practice showing love toward others by helping those in need, offering kind words, and being supportive in difficult times.

My Prayer Today

Conclude each entry by writing a short prayer, asking the Lord to help you apply His Word to your daily life.

_____

_____

_____

_____

_____

_____

Day 4

A Prayer for Love

Deuteronomy 7:9 KJV

Know therefore that the LORD thy God, he is God, the faithful God, which keeps covenant and mercy with them that love him and keep his commandments to a thousand generations;

Write a prayer about the love you want, need, or share with others in your life. Reflect on Psalms 143:8 and Deuteronomy 7:9 as you write your prayer.

_____

_____

_____

_____

_____

_____

_____

_____

_____

_____

DAY 5

Blessings of God

Numbers 6:24-25 KJV

> The LORD bless thee, and keep thee: The LORD make his face shine upon thee, and be gracious unto thee:

What are some ways we can receive Gods blessings according to The Word of God?

_____

_____

_____

_____

_____

Finish the scripture: O taste and see that the LORD is good: Blessed is the

_____ _____ in _____.

The scripture Psalm 34:8 encourages believers to experience God's goodness and trust in Him. How can you make this a part of your daily life?

_____

_____

_____

_____

_____

_____

_____

Here are some examples you can start your day with: a prayer of gratitude. You can also reflect on a verse during your lunch break or end your day by journaling about moments you felt God's presence.

The Word of God says they that be of faith are blessed with the faithful Abraham. This means that those who have faith are blessed just as Abraham was because of his faithfulness to God. What does this mean to you?

_____

_____

_____

_____

_____

_____

What did you learn about God's blessings?

_____

_____

_____

_____

_____

_____

Are you on the right path to receive God's blessings?

_____

If you answered yes to the previous question, how do you know this is true?

_____

_____

_____

If you answered no, how will you seek God's blessing?

_____

_____

_____

My Prayer Today

Conclude each entry by writing a short prayer, asking the Lord to help you apply His Word to your daily life.

_____

_____

_____

_____

_____

_____

_____

Day 6

Walking in Integrity

Proverbs 20:7 KJV

The just man walketh in his integrity: His children are blessed after him.

What is integrity in your own words, and how do you see it applied in everyday life?

_____

_____

_____

_____

_____

_____

What does God say about integrity in the scripture?

_____

_____

_____

_____

_____

_____

Explain Proverbs 11:3 by discussing how integrity guides the upright and prevents them from falling into dishonesty.

_____

_____

_____

_____

_____

_____

_____

My Prayer Today

Conclude each entry by writing a short prayer, asking the Lord to help you apply His Word to your daily life.

_____

_____

_____

_____

_____

_____

_____

Day 7

Favor from God

Proverbs 3:3-4 KJV

Let not mercy and truth forsake thee: Bind them about thy neck; Write them upon the table of thine heart: So shalt thou find favor and good understanding in the sight of God and man.

Proverbs 8:35 states, "Those who find me find life and receive God's favor."

Based on the reflective passage, how do we find God?

_____

_____

_____

_____

_____

What does Proverbs 8:35 say a good man receives from God?

_____

What occurs as we mature in our spiritual journey with God?

_____

_____

_____

_____

_____

_____

How do we grow in the things of God? What steps can we take to deepen our faith and spiritual practices?

_____

_____

_____

_____

_____

Which scripture about Gods favor in this devotion stood out to you the most?

_____

_____

_____

Based on the previous question: Did it speak to your spirit? If yes, describe how it did. If no, why did you pick this scripture?

_____

_____

_____

_____

_____

_____

My Prayer Today

Conclude each entry by writing a short prayer, asking the Lord to help you apply His Word to your daily life.

_____

_____

_____

_____

_____

Day 8

I Will Be Healthy

3 John 1:2 KJV

Beloved, I wish above all things that thou mayest prosper and be in health, even as thy soul prospers.

How do you interpret the above verse in relation to health?

_____

_____

_____

_____

_____

What forms of healing does God provide for us?

_____

_____

_____

_____

_____

Was it God's desire for us to be sick? Explore the Bible and today's devotion to explain why or why not.

_____

_____

_____

_____

Why is it essential to be deliberate with our words regarding healing?

_____

_____

_____

_____

List some words that you can speak over yourself for healing such as "I am strong," "I am healthy," "I am resilient," "I am at peace."

_____   _____

_____   _____

_____   _____

_____   _____

Which scriptures regarding healing can be applied throughout life?

_____

_____

_____

_____

_____

My Prayer Today

Conclude each entry by writing a short prayer, asking the Lord to help you apply His Word to your daily life.

_____

_____

_____

_____

_____

_____

Day 9

The Divine Protection of God

Isaiah 54:17 KJV

No weapon that is formed against thee shall prosper; and every tongue that shall rise against thee in judgment thou shalt condemn. This is the heritage of the servants of the LORD, and their righteousness is of me, saith the LORD.

What does God's protection mean to you?

_____

_____

_____

_____

_____

List two scriptures about God's protection.

_____

_____

_____

_____

_____

Why should we not rely on our own strength alone when dealing with daily issues, emotional or mental challenges?

_____

_____

_____

_____

_____

The promises of _____ are true and _____, let us follow the examples He has put in place for us, so that we will never _____ out of _____.

My Prayer Today

Conclude each entry by writing a short prayer, asking the Lord to help you apply His Word to your daily life.

_____

_____

_____

_____

_____

Day 10

Gods Sufficiency of His Grace

2 Corinthians 12:9 KJV

And he said to me, "My grace is sufficient for thee: for my strength is made perfect in weakness." Most gladly therefore will I rather glory in my infirmities, that the power of Christ may rest upon me.

My grace is sufficient for thee. This scripture, found in 2 Corinthians 12:9 is part of Paul's letter to the Corinthians where he discusses his struggles and God's reassurance. How has this scripture resonated with you in your own life?

_____

_____

_____

_____

_____

How can we receive God's grace?

_____

_____

_____

_____

Why are we given grace? Grace is often seen as an unearned favor or kindness that we receive despite our shortcomings.

_____

_____

_____

_____

How do you personally experience and understand God's grace in your life?

_____

_____

_____

_____

Which scripture reflects God's grace to you?

_____

_____

_____

_____

My Prayer Today

Conclude each entry by writing a short prayer, asking the Lord to help you apply
His Word to your daily life.

_____

_____

_____

_____

_____

_____

Day 11

Freedom from Sin

Romans 6:14 KJV

For sin shall not have dominion over you: for ye are not under the law, but under grace.

What is sin?

_____

_____

_____

_____

How do we overcome sin within our lives?

_____

_____

_____

_____

Why is it important to bring our wrongdoings into the light instead of hiding them?

_____

_____

_____

_____

_____

_____

What does it mean when we recognize something is wrong yet still choose to do it?

_____

_____

_____

List the works of the flesh.

_____   _____

_____   _____

_____   _____

_____   _____

_____   _____

_____   _____

How can you avoid practicing the works of the flesh listed above?

_____

_____

_____

_____

Why does Scripture warn us against being double-minded?

_____

_____

_____

The wages of sin are _____.

Can a person truly please God if their heart and actions are against Him? _____.
Share your thoughts.

_____

_____

_____

_____

Is temptation something that comes from God? _____ Explain
your thoughts.

_____

_____

_____

_____

_____

_____

How can being consumed with worldly things pull us away from God?

_____

_____

_____

_____

What became of our old sinful nature when we were crucified with Christ?

_____

_____

_____

_____

My Prayer Today

Conclude each entry by writing a short prayer, asking the Lord to help you apply His Word to your daily life.

_____

_____

_____

_____

_____

_____

Day 12

Faith in God

Hebrews 11:1 KJV

Now faith is the substance of things hoped for, the evidence of things not seen.

2 Corinthians 5:7 KJV

For we walk by faith, not by sight

How would you describe faith in your own words?

_____

_____

_____

_____

What happens when faith is absent in a believer's life?

_____

_____

_____

How have you personally integrated faith within your daily life?

_____

_____

_____

_____

_____

What are the benefits of having faith?

_____

_____

_____

_____

_____

What makes walking by faith more reliable than walking by sight?

_____

_____

_____

_____

_____

How can we build faith in God?

_____

_____

_____

_____

What is one example of how you've had to exercise faith recently?

_____

_____

_____

_____

List the things we can receive by having faith in God.

_____

_____

_____

_____

List 3 scriptures of faith that can help you with your walk with God.

_____

_____

_____

_____

According to Scripture, when we put our faith in God, with whom are we blessed?

_____

_____

_____

My Prayer Today

Conclude each entry by writing a short prayer, asking the Lord to help you apply His Word to your daily life.

_____

_____

_____

_____

_____

_____

Day 13

Intentional Prayer Life

Matthew 6:6 KJV

> *But, when you pray enter into your closet, and when you have shut the door, pray to the Father which is in secret; and your Father which see in secret shall reward you openly.*

Why is it necessary to be intentional in our prayer life?

_____

_____

_____

_____

According to Scripture, how are we instructed to pray?

_____

_____

_____

_____

Where is prayer able to take place?

_____

_____

_____

_____

Does the place of prayer matter as much as the posture of your heart?

_____

_____

_____

When you pray, what should you offer to God?

_____

_____

_____

When you approach God in prayer, what should your first words or focus be?

_____

_____

_____

According to Scripture, what are we called to believe when we pray?

_____

_____

_____

_____

How can you create an atmosphere of prayer wherever you are?

_____

_____

_____

_____

My Prayer Today

Conclude each entry by writing a short prayer, asking the Lord to help you apply His Word to your daily life.

_____

_____

_____

_____

_____

Day 14

Prayer For Job Opportunity & Leading

Proverbs 16:3 KJV

Commit thy works unto the LORD, and thy thoughts shall be established.

God knows the desire of our heart whether _____ or _____.

According to Scripture, what has God called His people to do?

_____

_____

_____

Scripture calls us to submit our works to the Lord. What does this involve?

_____

_____

_____

_____

What happens in our lives when we continually acknowledge God?

_____

_____

_____

_____

_____

_____

As you read, which passage of Scripture felt most personal to you?

_____

_____

_____

_____

_____

Spend a quiet moment thinking and praying over that scripture/s.

My Prayer Today

Conclude each entry by writing a short prayer, asking the Lord to help you apply His Word to your daily life.

_____

_____

_____

Day 15

Prayer To Be a Good Example for My Children & Those I Influence

John 14:6 KJV

Jesus saith unto him, I am the way, the truth, and the life: no man comes unto the Father, but by me.

Colossians 1:10 KJV

That you might walk worthy of the Lord unto all pleasing, being fruitful in every good work, and increasing in the knowledge of God.

According to Scripture, when we accept Jesus Christ as Lord and Savior, to whom are we led?

_____

_____

_____

_____

According to God's Word, who should we strive to please, and why is this important?

_____

_____

_____

_____

_____

To serve God it to _____ to _____.

In your own words, what does this mean to you?

_____

_____

_____

_____

What does choosing Christ require you to be?

_____

_____

_____

_____

My Prayer Today

Conclude each entry by writing a short prayer, asking the Lord to help you apply His Word to your daily life.

_____

_____

_____

_____

_____

_____

Day 16

Let Everyone Praise God

Hebrews 13:15 KJV

By him therefore let us offer the sacrifice of praise to God continually, that is, the fruit of our lips giving thanks to his name.

How would you define praise?

_____

_____

_____

_____

_____

How can we express praise?

_____

_____

_____

_____

_____

What does it show when we praise God?

_____

_____

_____

_____

What blessings or changes come as a result of praising God?

_____

_____

_____

_____

Praise is honoring the attributes of God. Write down the attributes Scripture reveals about Him.

_____

_____

_____

What is the difference between praise and worship?

_____

_____

_____

_____

_____

_____

Who should praise God?

_____

_____

When should we praise God?

_____

_____

How should we praise God?

_____

_____

What should we praise God for?

_____

_____

How can you make praise a consistent part of your daily life?

_____

_____

_____

_____

_____

My Prayer Today

Conclude each entry by writing a short prayer, asking the Lord to help you apply His Word to your daily life.

_____

_____

_____

_____

_____

Day 17

A Spouse from the Lord

Genesis 2:24 KJV

Therefore, shall a man leave his father and his mother and shall cleave unto his wife and they shall be one flesh.

According to Scripture, what was God's first instruction concerning marriage?

_____

_____

_____

How would you describe the meaning of "cleave" when God uses it to speak about marriage?

_____

_____

_____

_____

According to God's Word, how are husbands and wives called to unite?

_____

_____

_____

_____

_____

_____

Why are we encouraged to submit to each other?

_____

_____

_____

_____

Which spouse is instructed to show love in the same way Christ loves the church?

_____

_____

According to God's Word, how is marriage portrayed?

_____

_____

_____

What does the covenant of marriage signify to you in your walk with God?

_____

_____

_____

_____

According to Scripture, what instruction does Colossians 3:18–19 convey about marriage?

_____

_____

_____

_____

My Prayer Today

Conclude each entry by writing a short prayer, asking the Lord to help you apply His Word to your daily life.

_____

_____

_____

_____

_____

_____

_____

_____

Day 18

A Prayer for Guidance

Psalm 25:4-6 KJV

Shew me thy ways, O LORD; Teach me thy paths. Lead me in thy truth and teach me: For thou art the God of my salvation; on thee do I wait all the day. Remember, O LORD, thy tender mercies and thy loving kindness. For they have been ever of old

Show me the right path Lord and point out the road for me to follow.

How do we receive guidance from God?

_____

_____

_____

What is stated in Proverbs 3:5-6?

_____

_____

_____

_____

What does God's guidance point you toward in life?

_____

_____

_____

_____

_____

According to Scripture, what occurs when there is no guidance?

_____

_____

_____

_____

How would you summarize the message of Psalm 119:133?

_____

_____

_____

_____

How can Psalm 119:133 be applied in daily life?

_____

_____

_____

_____

What makes it necessary to turn to God for guidance each day?

_____

_____

_____

_____

How has God's guidance shaped the direction of your life, and how can you trust Him more fully with your next steps?

_____

_____

_____

_____

My Prayer Today

Conclude each entry by writing a short prayer, asking the Lord to help you apply His Word to your daily life.

_____

_____

_____

_____

_____

_____

Day 19

Help Me Not to Stumble Jesus

Jude 1:24-25 ASV

Now unto him that is able to guard you from stumbling, and to set you before the presence of his glory without blemish in exceeding joy, to the only God our Savior, through Jesus Christ our Lord, be glory, majesty, dominion and power, before all time, and now, and for evermore. Amen.

What does it mean to stumble spiritually?

_____

_____

_____

_____

When we walk in God's ways, what are we kept from?

_____

According to Scripture, why must believers seek sound wisdom and discernment?

_____

_____

_____

In what ways does living in obedience to God prevent spiritual stumbling?

_____

_____

_____

_____

How does exercising control over what you say and do impact your life and others?

_____

_____

_____

_____

How would you explain the message of Matthew 18:8–9?

_____

_____

_____

_____

What does this passage teach you about the seriousness of sin in your life?

_____

_____

_____

_____

What are some practical ways to live out the message of Matthew 18:8–9 each day?

_____

_____

_____

_____

What are the areas in your life where you are most prone to stumble, and how can you lean on God's strength to overcome them?

_____

_____

_____

_____

My Prayer Today

Conclude each entry by writing a short prayer, asking the Lord to help you apply His Word to your daily life.

_____

_____

_____

_____

_____

_____

Day 20

A Sound Mind

2 Timothy 1:7 KJV

For God has not given us the spirit of fear; but of power, and of love, and of a sound mind.

God has given us a sound mind.

What does it mean to have a sound mind?

_____

_____

_____

_____

_____

What does Proverbs 14:30 teach us about having a sound mind?

_____

_____

_____

_____

_____

What practices help you maintain a sound and peaceful mind?

_____

_____

_____

_____

What makes daily renewal of the mind so important for a believer?

_____

_____

_____

_____

How does Philippians 4:7 describe the effect of God's peace on our minds?

_____

_____

_____

_____

According to Scripture, how does living a purified life support a sound mind?

_____

_____

_____

_____

_____

What things tend to disturb your inner peace, and how can you surrender them to God?

_____

_____

_____

_____

How can you daily depend on God to strengthen and preserve a sound mind in every area of your life?

_____

_____

_____

_____

Meditate on Philippians 4:8

My Prayer Today

Conclude each entry by writing a short prayer, asking the Lord to help you apply His Word to your daily life.

_____

_____

_____

_____

_____

_____

Day 21

The God of Hope

Romans 15:13 KJV

Now the God of hope fill you with all joy and peace in believing, that ye may abound in hope, through the power of the Holy Ghost.

How would you define hope?

_____

_____

_____

_____

In what ways can you live out hope each day?

_____

_____

_____

_____

How would you complete the phrase: "God is the God of..."?

_____

_____

In what ways does God provide help for us to remain hopeful?

_____

_____

_____

What happens when we live with eager expectation in hope?

_____

_____

_____

What does the last passage teach us about hope?

_____

_____

_____

_____

What makes it important to be prepared to share the reason for your hope?

_____

_____

_____

_____

_____

How can you keep your hope anchored in God through every season of life?

_____

_____

_____

_____

My Prayer Today

Conclude each entry by writing a short prayer, asking the Lord to help you apply His Word to your daily life.

_____

_____

_____

_____

Day 22

The Miracle Power of God

Luke 18:27 KJV

And He said, the things which are impossible with men are possible with God.

What does the above scripture reveal to you about God?

_____

_____

_____

_____

How can we experience God's power at work in our lives?

_____

_____

_____

_____

According to Scripture, what keeps miracles from happening in our lives?

_____

_____

_____

_____

Why is it important to believe God's Word?

_____

_____

_____

_____

Is it possible for believers to have the power to perform miracles? Why or why not?

_____

_____

_____

_____

How can you live each day with greater faith and expectation in God's miracle-working power?

_____

_____

_____

_____

My Prayer Today

Conclude each entry by writing a short prayer, asking the Lord to help you apply His Word to your daily life.

_____

_____

_____

_____

_____

Day 23

The Strength of God

Philippians 4:13 KJV

I can do all things through Christ which strengthens me.

How would you describe the above scripture in your own words?

_____

_____

_____

_____

What are some examples of strength?

_____

_____

_____

How would you define strength?

_____

_____

_____

How is strength understood in a biblical context?

_____

_____

_____

_____

What makes trusting God essential when it comes to finding strength?

_____

_____

_____

_____

Which verses from today's devotion will you lean on when you need strength?

_____

_____

_____

_____

What happens when we rely on God.

_____

_____

_____

_____

_____

_____

Which scripture tells us that the Lord gives strength to His people and bless His people with peace.

_____

Remember to use the meditation scriptures to help strengthen you.

How can you depend on God's strength rather than your own in the challenges you face each day?

_____

_____

_____

_____

My Prayer Today

Conclude each entry by writing a short prayer, asking the Lord to help you apply His Word to your daily life.

_____

_____

_____

_____

_____

_____

_____

_____

Day 24

The Strong Hold of God

Nahum 1:7 KJV

*The Lord is good, **a strong hold in the day of trouble**; and He knows them that trust in Him.*

How would you interpret the meaning of the verse referenced above?

_____

_____

_____

_____

God is our stronghold. In what ways is God a stronghold for you?

_____

_____

_____

_____

Why is it important to remember God in all that we do and face daily?

_____

_____

_____

_____

How should we fight our battles?

_____

_____

_____

_____

What weapons are used to fight the battles we face daily?

_____

_____

_____

_____

Isaiah 41:10 tell us to "fear not". Why is it important after reading the entire scripture for us not to be fearful?

_____

_____

_____

_____

How does knowing that God is your strong hold in times of trouble give you comfort and security?

_____

_____

_____

_____

In what ways have you experienced God's goodness as your strong hold during difficult seasons?

_____

_____

_____

_____

What area of your life right now most needs the assurance that God is your strong hold?

_____

_____

_____

_____

My Prayer Today

Conclude each entry by writing a short prayer, asking the Lord to help you apply His Word to your daily life.

_____

_____

_____

_____

_____

_____

Day 25

Bind Loose Decree Declare Receive

Ephesians 6:12 KJV

For we wrestle not against flesh and blood, but against principalities, against powers, against the rulers of the darkness of this world, against spiritual wickedness in high places.

Matthew 16:19 KJV

I will give you the keys to the kingdom of heaven; whatever you bind on earth will be bound in heaven, and whatever you loose on earth will be loosed in heaven.

What does it mean that we do not wrestle against flesh and blood?

_____

_____

_____

What does the Bible teach us about resisting and overcoming principalities?

_____

_____

_____

_____

_____

_____

Which key has been placed in the hands of believers, and what does it represent?

_____

_____

_____

How does binding on earth affect what happens in the spiritual realm?

_____

_____

_____

According to Scripture, what takes place when believers loose things through prayer on earth?

_____

_____

_____

According to Psalm 73:28, what truth is revealed about drawing near to God?

_____

_____

_____

_____

_____

_____

Luke 10:19 tells us that God has given us power to do what?

_____

_____

_____

Why is being sober-minded important?

_____

_____

_____

_____

2 Thessalonians 3:3 says what?

_____

_____

_____

_____

How can you apply the authority of binding and loosing in your daily walk with God?

_____

_____

_____

_____

My Prayer Today

Conclude each entry by writing a short prayer, asking the Lord to help you apply His Word to your daily life.

_____

_____

_____

_____

_____

_____

Day 26

With Thanksgiving

1 Thessalonians 5:18 KJV

In everything give thanks: for this is the will of God in Christ Jesus concerning you.

According to Scripture, why does God instruct us to give thanks in everything?

_____

_____

_____

_____

_____

What does it mean to be grateful in all things?

_____

_____

_____

_____

Thankfulness expresses what to God?

_____

_____

_____

_____

Ephesians 5:20 reminds us of what?

_____

_____

_____

How should we enter the presence of God?

_____

_____

_____

What does **Gate** represent in Psalm 100:4?

_____

_____

_____

_____

_____

_____

Why is it important to allow the peace of God in our hearts?

_____

_____

_____

_____

_____

If everything God created is _____, why should it not be refused.

Psalms 69:30 say.

_____

_____

_____

_____

How can you live each day with a heart of thanksgiving, giving thanks in all circumstances as God commands?

_____

_____

_____

_____

_____

My Prayer Today

Conclude each entry by writing a short prayer, asking the Lord to help you apply
His Word to your daily life.

_____

_____

_____

_____

_____

_____

Day 27

Rejuvenation

Jeremiah 31:25 KJV

For I have satiated the weary soul, and I have replenished every sorrowful soul.

What does it mean to satiate the weary soul?

_____

_____

_____

_____

What does replenish mean?

_____

_____

_____

_____

Why is rejuvenation important for all believers?

_____

_____

_____

_____

What are some ways to refresh ourselves?

_____

_____

_____

_____

Who is meant to guide our lives?

_____

_____

_____

_____

To whom should we entrust our burdens?

_____

_____

_____

_____

Let us continue in today's lesson and recite the 2 scriptures given to us, so that we release everything to God and renew our minds.

My Prayer Today

Conclude each entry by writing a short prayer, asking the Lord to help you apply His Word to your daily life.

_____

_____

_____

_____

_____

_____

Day 28

My God, My Provision, My Needs

Philippians 4:19 KJV

But my God shall supply all your needs according to His riches in glory by Christ Jesus.

What does it look like for God to provide for all our needs?

_____

_____

_____

_____

_____

What are some instances of God supplying your needs?

_____

_____

_____

_____

_____

In what ways are God's riches shown to us?

_____

_____

_____

_____

What does it take to have our needs supplied by God?

_____

_____

_____

_____

What does Malachi 3:10 reveal about the practice of tithing?

_____

_____

_____

_____

What does Proverbs 3:9-10 say about honoring God?

_____

_____

_____

_____

_____

_____

Luke 6:38 says "give and it will be given to you." How does it describe the way we will receive?

_____

_____

_____

_____

What does Proverbs 10:22 tell us?

_____

_____

_____

_____

Complete the verse: But seek ye first the kingdom of God and His

_____ and all _____ _____ shall

be _____ unto _____. (Matthew 6:33)

My Prayer Today

Conclude each entry by writing a short prayer, asking the Lord to help you apply His Word to your daily life.

_____

_____

_____

_____

_____

_____

Day 29

Love, Knowledge & Discernment

Philippians 1:9 KJV

And this I pray, that your love may abound yet more and more in knowledge and in all judgement.

Love

John 3:16 shows us God's great love. How did He demonstrate that love?

_____

_____

_____

_____

How does the second passage describe God's love living in us?

_____

_____

_____

_____

_____

What does 1 John 4:8 tell us?

_____

_____

_____

_____

Can you give an example of how this could appear in our lives?

_____

_____

_____

_____

Knowledge & Discernment

How does studying the Word of God increase our knowledge?

_____

_____

_____

_____

At what point do we gain discernment?

_____

_____

_____

What does Gods Word accomplish?

_____

_____

_____

What message do we find in Proverbs 18:15?

_____

_____

_____

How can we apply this in our daily lives?

_____

_____

_____

_____

_____

_____

My Prayer Today

Conclude each entry by writing a short prayer, asking the Lord to help you apply His Word to your daily life.

_____

_____

_____

_____

_____

_____

Day 30

Divine Wisdom & Understanding

Colossians 1:9 KJV

For this cause we also, since the day we heard it, do not cease to pray for you, and to desire that you might be filled with knowledge of His will in all wisdom and spiritual understanding.

How is the beginning of wisdom described?

_____

_____

_____

_____

How do we gain the knowledge of God?

_____

_____

_____

_____

What does the third passage say about understanding?

_____

_____

_____

_____

_____

How do Proverbs 2:6-8 describe God's role in giving wisdom and protection?

_____

_____

_____

_____

What is the contrast between worldly wisdom and God's wisdom?

_____

_____

_____

_____

Can you give some examples of worldly wisdom?

_____

_____

_____

_____

_____

_____

Can you give some examples of Godly wisdom?

_____

_____

_____

_____

What priority does Proverbs 4:7 set for us?

_____

_____

_____

_____

Complete the scripture Proverbs 3:13: _____ is the _____ that

finds _____, and the _____ that gets

_____.

My Prayer Today

Conclude each entry by writing a short prayer, asking the Lord to help you apply His Word to your daily life.

_____

_____

_____

_____

_____

_____

Day 31

The Peace & Joy of God

Romans 15:13 KJV

Now the God of hope fill you with all joy and peace in believing, that you may abound in hope, through the power of the Holy Ghost.

Joy: A deep gladness of the heart that comes from God's presence, not dependent on circumstances.

Peace: A steady calm and inner stillness, rooted in trust in God and His promises.

How do we obtain the joy and peace that comes from God?

_____

_____

_____

_____

How can we discern that our peace is really from God? What are some examples of this?

_____

_____

_____

_____

_____

_____

Why is trusting God essential for true peace?

_____

_____

_____

_____

What does John 14:27 tell us Jesus left for us?

_____

_____

_____

_____

How does Philippians 4:4 call us to respond?

_____

_____

_____

_____

As believers, what should we always be full of, and what should we be doing?

_____

_____

_____

_____

What does Jesus tell us in John 15:9?

_____

_____

_____

_____

How would you explain Isaiah 55:12?

_____

_____

_____

_____

_____

How does trusting in God fill your life with His peace and joy, even in challenging times?

_____

_____

_____

_____

What step can you take to rely more on the power of the Holy Spirit to fill you with peace, joy, and hope?

_____

_____

_____

My Prayer Today

Conclude each entry by writing a short prayer, asking the Lord to help you apply His Word to your daily life.

_____

_____

_____

_____

_____

Final Blessing

As you complete these 31 days of reflection, remember that God's Word is living and active. Each page you have written is more than ink on paper it is a record of your journey with Him. May the truths you have discovered continue to guide your steps, strengthen your faith, and draw you closer to the heart of God. May His Spirit remind you daily that His Word never returns void but always accomplishes what He intends.

Continuing the Journey

- Revisit this workbook with fresh eyes repeat the 31 days using different verses or themes.
- Choose one scripture from these pages each week to memorize and pray over.
- Use these reflections in small groups, Bible studies, or personal quiet time.
- Keep journaling daily, even beyond this workbook, to capture what God is speaking to your heart.

Prayer Tracker

Use this section to record your prayer requests, answered prayers, and moments of gratitude.

Date	Prayer Request	Scripture to Stand On	Answered (✓)	Notes of Praise

Reflection Summary

At the end of this journey, pause to consider what God has done.

The biggest truth I learned through this workbook:

_____

_____

A habit I want to continue:

_____

_____

A scripture I will carry with me:

_____

_____

A prayer I will keep praying:

_____

_____

Notes

Notes

About the Author

Nadia A. L. Farrington is a Christian committed to helping believers grow in their walk with God by understanding and applying His Word. Through her devotionals and resources, she seeks to make Scripture practical and life-giving. She writes with a gentle, encouraging voice, inspiring readers to deepen their faith through prayer, reflection, and daily obedience.

Stay Connected

Your walk with God is a lifelong journey and we can walk it together.

Connect with Nadia:

🌐 www.whispersatsunrise.com

TikTok: whispers.at.sunri

📱 Instagram: @WhispersAtSunrise2025

📖 Download free Bible study resources at

www.whispersatsunrise.com

✉️ Join my email list for devotionals and updates.

🎥 Follow faith-building content on TikTok, YouTube, and Instagram.

Other books & resources by Nadia A. L. Farrington:

- *Thus Says The Lord Devotional*
- *Whispers at Sunrise: A 30-Day Guided Prayer Journal*
- *A Temple Made Holy: Becoming a Living Sanctuary for the Holy Spirit*

www.ingramcontent.com/pod-product-compliance
Lightning Source LLC
Chambersburg PA
CBHW080019130626
46556CB00016B/3251